Myths of Electricity

Myths of Electricity

Kevin Meaux

Texas Review Press
Huntsville, Texas

FIRST EDITION, 2005

Requests for permission to reproduce material from this work should be sent to:

> Permissions
> Texas Review Press
> English Department
> Sam Houston State University
> Huntsville, TX 77341-2146

Acknowledgments:

Some of the poems in this volume have been published by the following magazines, some of them in slightly altered versions:

> *Image: A Journal of Arts and Religion*
> *Poetry*
> *Prairie Schooner*
> *Shenandoah*
> *Southeast Review*
> *Southern Humanities Review*
> *Southern Review*
> *Southwest Review*
> *21st: The Journal of Contemporary Photography*

Many of these poems were written under a generous fellowship from The Louisiana Division of the Arts as well as Poetry Magazine's Ruth Lilly Fellowship. I could not be more grateful. I also want to thank the following individuals for their friendship, critical/editorial skills, and wisdom: Morri Creech, John Wood, Neil Connelly, Damon and Cassie Falke, Holly Carrie, Lawrence Turner, and Michelle Ritter.

Library of Congress Cataloging-in-Publication Data
Meaux, Kevin, 1969-
  Myths of electricity / Kevin Meaux.-- 1st ed.
      p. cm.
  ISBN 1-881515-73-7 (alk. paper)
  I. Title.
  PS3613.E19M98 2005
  811'.6--dc22

                                                                    20050136

For Ashlynn Ivy

Contents

Myths of Electricity

The Dusk of Uncles

1. Flame

My uncles often talked of it.
Cornfields caught fire.
Winds kindled the pasture grass
till barns and tree lines ignited. It was a story
they'd pass around the back porch,
perfecting the details
of that season cinder drifted
thick as evening,
settled in wells—drawn water
tasted of smoke, they said,
and birds fell smoldering
into embered fields. And maybe
it's all true: how fire took the town,
how after the salvaging—
the beams and hearthstones
hoisted from ashheaps—some claimed
they'd seen lightning blast the corn crop,
though my uncles promised
it was one of the cousins, gone gasoline-happy
and hungry for judgment day.

2. Sickness

And what of the farm daughter,
that same summer, waking fevered
as rabies bristled in her blood?
They told me she lay seven days
in a palsied room, that her parents
tried to conjure some angel
or patron saint, tried even the cures
of country healers, burning garlic stalks
and wreaths of sweetbroom
before a shotgun stilled her frenzy.

3. Mystery

My uncles often talked
of such things. And I wondered
why their tales led always
to sickness or cinders,
whirling blades and chainsaws,
or limbs ground up in gears.
I still think of their stories,
how they sat there recounting lives
mangled in machinery
and all those children
curious for stray dogs
and shining jars of arsenic.
These were the mysteries
my uncles pondered like prayer beads,
repeating this or that disaster
until the air seemed alchemized
by their evening talk and swirled bourbon,
their liturgies of grief
beneath the back porch stars.

Thoughts on Human Beauty in the Y Locker Room

You might ponder what the Maker had in mind
once the shucked clothes collapse
and shower heads hiss and billow out the balm of warm fog
upon us all, our stomachs' harrowed bags,
the spinal knobs rising in their bowed columns,
the chests now sunken or slung with dugs.
What Eve would ever dream of us? And where
in so much glow of grouted tile do Whitman's bathers hide?
No doubt you'll note that scar's puckered gully,
the scarlet birthmark sprawling map-shaped
and shoulder blades pocked with constellations.
Difficult to picture some unseen hand
following droplets down those ribs' thin pickets.
Yet here are the figures, the forms on parchment,
drawn for centuries in Vitruvian balance
or crafted into Adam on chapel ceilings, his torso hard as
    armor.
Think of Eden, fixed in a frieze: the Lord's garden
where stone boughs hang, their apples
half-forgotten beside the bared paradigm of belly and thigh.
So it is that you might notice, finally,
amid the sodden towels and cloud-slickened mirrors,
how the flesh undrapes its pale revelations,
though who among us shall gauge from such bodies
the golden ratios of grace or calculate each part into praise?
Here the heavens shed a harsh fluorescence,
revealing the least stipples of blemish on blanched hips,
on limbs and backs no master's carved in quarried marble,
fallen as we are from that garden of clear and chiseled
    symmetries.

Snake Handling

I remember them winding
through high weeds and thicket,
their yield and push
among fallen locust leaves.
My cousin pretended faith
as he plucked them up,
swung them until they hummed
and blurred the bright air.
He told me of churches
where snakes rolled like oil
over scarred knuckles,
where people prayed with poison
and sang in the tounges
of cottonmouths and copperheads.
He took up snakes
as if among the faithful
whose prayers shook them
and toppled their bodies
from the spirit's balcony.
He cracked them like wet rope
against tree trunks
and flung their snapped flesh
into the fallow field,
spun them upward into limbs
where they hung
beneath the preaching of waxwings.
And when I knelt,
touching the head
torn clean from its body,
I saw the satin jaws
open like a last thought,
striking miracle into my hand.

Nikola Tesla in Budapest, 1881

The particular malady that now affected him was never diagnosed. One of the symptoms was an acute sensitivity of all the sense organs...this sensitivity was so tremendously exaggerated that its effects were a form of torture.
   —John J. O'Neal, **Prodigal Genius: The Life of Nikola Tesla**

I felt daylight flame beneath my skin.
The burning circuits of my veins
mapped each muscle.

I could scarcely stand the air,
its prickling static—
friction of dust and filament.

And for weeks
I lay in padded darkness.
Each Sunday
when the sound of church bells pounded,
memory's waves rang through me:
I was the child
who watched his father rehearse sermons,
who climbed the bell tower
and pulled ropes in the rung sunlight
as rafters exploded with birds.

But how wrong I was
to fear and praise that dim god.

My father's myths and hymns
told nothing of the ignited Christ,
God of the Charge
who gives no redemption.
My nerves have felt His currents,
the coil of His fury.
The universe crackles,
and all His thoughts combust into spun stars.

On Visiting a Childhood Home

For Morri Creech

As always, the summer unreels into wisteria
and dense clumps of honeysuckle, enthralling the backyard
    bees.
I'd nearly swear that nothing's changed
as the workshed lets out its long breath of burnt oil and
    sawdust
and tree spiders work their silken equations between the
    boughs.

And what does it matter, really,
if someone's hauled off the garden's border of bricks,
hacked away the mulberry
that for decades stained the driveway?—
because birds still weave their bowls in the greenhouse eaves
and, every summer, tangles of thorn barb the fenceline.

But maybe such lasting and sunlit fragments
beguile me to this yard where years ago my grandfather
stooped among the garlic stalks and parsley
or clipped a jar of hydrangea for the kitchen window.
And even here I have no claim to the past,
though its hold on me glimmers in the silk threads anchored
        to branches,
swells with the day's fragrance of cut grass, of honeysuckle
        and sawdust.

Impossible, yet we all know the shopworn wish
of spooling back the hours to their bobbin—compelling us
toward the mower's drone somewhere down the block,
backyards and bee-haunted gardens
where time spindled out the minutes of childhood,
where cicadas still rise and choir among the trees.

The Young Magician and His Wife

After a photograph of my parents, newly married

If one can believe such things,
the afternoon blushes
with summer's articulate brilliance
as my dad levitates my mom.

His hands are poised inches above her.
His eyes close in concentration
as if this were no trick
but a delicate task.

She's weightless and smiling.
Between her back and the ground
there is nothing but sunlight.

They're too young
to know what they're doing.
Soon she will settle into soft grass
or it will rise to meet her.
And so he concentrates
on his hands, his wife,
the bright bed of sunlight.

Hymn for Abandoned Things

Only when the gates are rusted shut
and paint flakes from the porch rails,
and thistle has its way
beneath the once-prim hibiscus;
only when the cellar's been pillaged
and the plumbing gutted,
and no scrollworked hinge or fixture's
left fastened to the walls—
only then can absence cast its grace
upon windows warping in their frames,
the bared halls and banisters,
the shelves emptied of heirloom silver.

So, too, we find a scrap yard's Babel
of stacked automobiles, or the town rice mill
with bins cleared and the sifters auctioned off.
A kind of afterlife, perhaps,
but hardly noticed along roadsides.
See the trailer now swaybacked in a gravel lot
and leaning barns lodged out to swallows.
Not to mention the junked hulls of johnboats
bleached from seasons on riverbanks.

Fair enough that weathers, at last,
collapse each beam and sagging rafter
while chassis go unsalvaged in the fields.
For nothing else but wreckage
could ever bless such a derelict heaven
of dust and sunlight, where things abandoned
lay broken, brittling toward their stripped essentials.
And whatever's neglected
will inherit the hushed corners of this kingdom,
as winds alone compose the low hymns
for all that's tarnished and born again among the weeds.

Landscapes and Omens

1.

I've heard how creatures common as swallows
feel floods coming, hail and cyclones,
how dogs howl hours before roofbeams buckle
and glasses rattle from the shelves,
how farm town prophets watch not for comets
or planets aligning, but study instead
columns of ants climbing the cypress,
blackbirds, like scattered smoke, lifting from wheat,
and fish dimpling the still surface of ponds: they say
such is the honeybee's knowledge as barometers drop
and continents grind miles beneath our feet—
truer than rheumatism, hip pins, or steel plates aching
when the future funnels down from clouds.

2.

Take my uncle, for instance,
who often swore he saw harbingers,
told me that even as gulf winds
helix into hurricane, brood mares kick
and cows give milk bitter as jimson weed.
Many Sundays I heard aunts and grandparents
tell of storm birds whirling inland,
cicadas gone quiet, their clamor in the trees
fallen to chapeled silence.

These were the women who scalded jars
and set the jam pots boiling,
cast their predictions
as spoons glistened, crystalling with sugar.
Their husbands, likewise,

knew what signs to watch—yearly signals
more certain to them than tillage,
than incense of burnt cane
hazing acres before the reaping.

3.

But no one's left in my family
to speak each season's dialect, the language
my uncles once culled from fields—
gossip of cotton rows withered,
breezes parched enough to scour the silos
and creekbeds dried to cobble.

And no one's left to believe
the landscape's revelations, those prophecies
of bough and birdwing,
though I still recall the voices
filling my grandparents' kitchen,
filling it with talk of harvests and warning,
tin roofs torn to razor
and whole barns blown heavenward.

4.

What's to be done
once our future funnels down
and the divinations
of ants and honeybees
prove useless—
once blackbirds fail to rise
like hieroglyphs,
no grammar of wingspan
wheeling upward into omens?

Such obvious logic
defies all warning: how time
spirals everything away,
tears plank from girder,
topples the house
where psalms and recipes
papered my grandmother's pantry.

Or maybe loss itself
redeems the details—
those Sabbath afternoons
I spent listening to kitchen talk—
as if winds could burnish
the trivia of years,
myths of weather and weeping statues,
could whip the flame-ripened fields
until the bright spires
quicken toward harvest.

Tesla on Immortality

This evening as I passed a chapel
the fragrance of candle wax and blossoms
blended with memories of my father
and childhood's iconed hours.
Hands pressed flat on the pulpit,
he'd lean in practiced rapture,
promising paradise and eternal life.
His tone was so low and glowing
that for a time I, too, believed.

And now they say even Edison,
inspired by séances,
devises gadgets to hear the dead speak—
radios receiving the short waves
of faith's frequencies.

But I would tell them both
that the soul, like breathing,
is a function of the flesh,
machinery of tendon and artery,
humming with electrical haloes,
blessed by vibration and flame.
Why foul the brief brilliance of such a temple,
trade its radiance for whispering spirits,
for psalms and the cupped blood of Christ?

Let memory alone resurrect the dead,
while graves, like fallen altars, go ignored,
attended only by sculpted angels
who gaze down, brooding
over the bare white logic of bones.

Fears and Early Mysteries

I first heard of walking spirits
in tales my cousins told—like the pickaxed woman
wandering the cemetery's gravel path;
or the drowned child, his ghost
rank as rotting fish and river mud;
or that house on the outskirts,
the one whose ruin rose amid willows
and where, to hear it told,
some husband was cleavered in his sleep.

I once feared those fables,
the meathooks and hatchets,
and the victims risen like mist.
How could I have known
the years would soon reveal
empty winds bickering through leaves
and stirring brambles along the riverbank?—
that soon I'd see the worst fears
turn quaint as late night movies,
the homicidal fathers
all corny as Karloff
stumbling up the cobwebbed stairs?

More than screeching doors
and footsteps in the hall,
it's the shadows passing
my bathroom mirror—
phantom lumps
or the omens of moles
darkening and shifting shape—
that fret the hours now. And some nights
I jog beside the graveyard
counting constellations
or watching moonlight pale the poplar tops,

afraid only of age
and how easily
we give up each mystery
until nothing's left,
no ghosts or gods,
no spirit rising
from its rubbled mansion
of breath and blood—nothing
but the stars' cold certainties.

My Grandfather's Trees

For years he tended them, mulberry and cedar,
and the crape myrtle squandering its blossoms across the
    yard—
until he could read each season's passage mapped amid the
    trees.

Or so it seems to me these days. We often hoisted the dead
    limbs,
uncoiled the poison vine from cut stumps and fence posts.
One August tent caterpillars wove the oaks in gossamer,
the bridal trunks lovely with spun veils of blight, though all
    month
my grandfather walked the yard with torches and cans of
    kerosene.

His was the kingdom where persimmons bent the profligate
    branches,
and figs, drenched with their own sweetness, rotted where they
    dropped
so that hornets hung in the grass and bees plundered the
    honeysuckle.
Most everything went to waste. Mottled pears melted into wet
    soil
and mockingbirds left plums half-ravaged on the bough.

Yet each summer the attic fan's great blades drew breezes
    weighted with maypop,
drew in the jasmined evenings to nectar the halls of my
    grandfather's house
while hard buds of starlight grew luminous among the leaves.
And so the hours conjured their pollen, dusting the fronds of
    hunched mimosas,
and whole years gave over to hawthorn's cast-off petals and
    air heavy with honey.

What's left but the language gathered from my grandfather's
    labor,
that rhetoric of sprawling shade and rainfall, of seasons
ripening thriftless on the stem? For decades he coaxed the
    slow workings
of root and resin, clipped the stricken branches and banked
    them for the flames
as blue jays called out their clamorous blessings in the weather.

Scenes from a Hometown

Notice these yards, the trucks rusting on cinderblocks,
and the Liberty Mill, its windows busted and doors boarded
    over.
Surely some deft elegist could distill and perfect praise or grief
from pastures where harrows collapse among the weeds
or from Main Street's billboards fading to a fine whitewash.

Here's the feedstore. My cousins and uncles
once garnered their harvest talk on its front porch,
daydreamed of sweet and countless acres pinnacling into cane
and fields bending with corn's bright coinage.

Of course, the church is unchanged. Beside the walkway
a grottoed Madonna consecrates her portion of primrose;
stone saints pray fixed in their postures, and footsteps hush
under the branches' canticles of breeze and birdsong.

But doesn't nostalgia stain everything here?—
even the trestled bridge at the town's outskirts
where the afternoon spends its odors of creosote and
    peppergrass,
or the barn that stores only its hoard of cracked axles,
hayrakes and winched engines slatted with sunlight.

Still, note these homes, the clapboards' paint blistering off in
    patches
as maypops scatter their prodigal blossoms along the
    hedgerows.
Every block's familiar in its solace of slow decline—
sidewalks broken where long ago the oak roots hove them up
and honey locusts bearing a thistled brilliance into the evening.

Bad Angels

Let us trust the better angels of our nature.

But what about the others,
those borne on wings of rising bile,
the bloody knuckled cherubs
who spiral us into anger? Often
I trust them when their rusted trumpets
blare off key. Yes, better to blame
gaggles of seraphic riff-raff
for times when average malice
fires into righteousness.
In those same blistering zones
where Christ tore through the temple,
I've cursed cashiers,
leaned hard on the car's horn
and driven my fist through doors.

What's to be made of them
when they come slouching from clouds,
the shabby angels of rage and regret?
I wince at their gifts.
They bring memories of grade school,
of hitting the fat kid
whose glasses fractured when he fell.
They assemble whole scenes,
each word cast at parents,
the gems and gleaming silver of guilt.

Yet what would we do
without their hurled turds and tempests?
Some might spend their limp years
marveling that even love's gone
bland as baby food. Others
will simper through streets

parading pastel flags,
while I, the old Tory of wrath,
sit with the shades drawn,
mutter pledges to celestial thugs
and dream of the lost order,
the storms that brought such bitter balance.

The Garden

I clear the garden of blown limbs
then work the dirt into furrows,
remembering the years my grandfather
leaned over this leverage of clumped root and shovel.
Each winter he waited
and thumbed the soiled pages of seed catalogues.
And though he had no use for the polished God,
no use, even in dying, for the logic of bread and spirit,
I know he spent those winters
planning a heaven dense with petals.

This morning I want to assemble a faith
from tangled branches piled high at the yard's corner,
compose prayer from the clear theorems of mineral
and the names
by which my grandfather knew each blossom.
I've seen withered mounds of foxglove
hallow the compost heap with fever.
The patience of decay
takes root and works through leaf and sepal.
Even the mind's great rooms of light
transform, cell by cell,
into darkness. And I want to believe
in a kingdom where nothing is saved,
where bees, like cast-out angels,
feed on the boughs of their bending temples.

Myths of Electricity: A Letter to Nikola Tesla

For John Wood

My cousin once claimed
he saw a tractor's axle
magnetized by lightning. I've heard too
of field hands found scorched,
the coins and keys fused in their pockets,
heard how splintered bolts
can burn a person's silhouette into the wall
or sizzle through miles of pipe and powerline
to set whole towns ablaze.

No wonder you bowed to such a god,
believing clouds housed fires brighter than Christ.
But what terrible and radiant angel did you invoke
when voltage arced from the spinning coil?

Jehovah gorged Himself on holy madmen
until their limbs went thin as kindling sticks.
How were you different from them?—penniless,
half-starved in your apartment, and talking to phantoms?

You often said the soul, like breathing,
is a function of the flesh,
said the body's mysteries veil mere machinery.
Yet you bent to the scripture of science,
saw a heaven that crackled with static and starlight,
and you paid, just like all those raving saints,
the cost of conjuring your insatiate god.

Southern Gothic

1.

Always the graveyard where the heft of history
cracks marble and mortar,
where, year through century, the chiseled names
bear their stories
and even the willow's thickest limb
splinters beneath the weight of rumor.
And forever the vacant lot, ragged with crabgrass,
that place where decades ago
some tale of outrage—a slung noose
or shotgun in the mouth—sank like blight into the soil.
Truth is, there's no sense
to this headstrong affection for shop-front gossip
and the hard talk of uncles, those old men
held mesmerized by their legends of lockjaw and arson.

2.

Or the farm house, for example, now empty,
where plaster saints and sun-washed angels haunt the lawn
and anyone listening might eavesdrop
on each creak of decay's drafty palaver in the attic.
Who wouldn't imagine a hacked husband
or headless bride walking such halls?—
as though a purgatory of floorboards and banisters
lay just beyond our logic.
                                  Consider, too,
the failed acres out back, the tractor's husk,
the harrow bound in snags of jasmine,
and how mystery's promise thrives here
in these fields long fallen to bramble's bare wreckage.

3.

Never the yards lined with prize camellias,
the Coin Laundry, or polished Chryslers outside the body
     shop;
never the town where mill whistles measure the hours
and the crop duster trails its cargo of cloud above the
     highway;

for that isn't the south whose broken boughs
drag always among the tattered stalks of goldenrod—
whose window panes rattle their half-truths
to the frayed veils of drapery, the cupboard's dusty shelves.

4.

This is the south built merely from whispered tales
passing across the porch or back pew,
though only a few of us now bother
recalling the talk that filled our kitchens at canning time
and drifted once upon the chapel's ether
of lit wicks and benedictions.
Even so, the lean fields lavish their harvest of hearsay
on town shop fronts and hewn benches beside the feed store,
and saints, of course, go on showing
their wounds of cracked plaster
as willows keep an unkempt vigil near the headstones—
all of it empty as wind's discourse
through attic rafters, through graveyards and vacant lots,
those landscapes washed always
by time's rich syntax of rumor and ruin.

A Prayer Against Heaven

In truth I'd rather some chaos had spun the dust of galaxies,
that chance alone, Lord, had set the planets coursing in their
        orbits.
And it's better the sparrow falls unheeded in the field.
Better still that gilded clouds drift emptied of angels.
For the fact is I'd rather that no garden
of myth-ridden boughs had ever meddled with our days,
and no hunger for heaven had swayed the imagination
from this world where grackles bless the air
with harsh calls and the blurred work of wingbeats,
and where the afternoon's wind-stripped leaves
twirl in brief cotillions across the lawn.
Strange, though, how Your kingdom beleaguers us
even as summer reveals its opulent logic among the trees;
and how You'd have us forsake the brazen flames
of wayside flowers, the river's glint,
the clear chill of stars locked in their constellations.
Oh, of course seasons ravage the branches
and blind hours cast each fattened apple to the ground.
But suppose I'd rather my own life
ripen toward that same obliteration. What penitence
should I feel, then, Lord? And what remorse
for the stubborn heart, faithful as it is to these flawed
        orchards,
these limbs housing the sovereign hives of honeybees?

Three Visions of Halley's Comet

In memory of my grandparents

1.

She stumbled past patches of melon and bindweed,
refused to look above
but saw His sign in the shadows of the gangly corn.
She'd arrive dust-blackened
and tell her parents the end was here,
that Christ was over the corn and had come as fire.
She'd press the children to her,
tell them to clamp shut their eyes
while His wrath washed the orchards,
burst the persimmons into raptures of burnt syrup
and steepled the cedars with flame.

She ran through the tall stalks,
envisioned horses battering the barnwood,
kicking loose the slats
as hay took the shape of burning,
and she imagined the cries of her father
as his farm fell and rose again
as fire, as the bright face of God.

2.

That night he dreamed of sitting
high in the hinged music of branches
and hearing the tail's pollen
patter the leaves.
He saw it cling to the fields
and the flowers of his father's garden,
saw the lattice lean heavy
with honeysuckle.

And he dropped from the limbs
to walk the deep powder,
and he knew the soil was seeded
with heaven,
that it would bloom row upon row
and rise from the compost
and soon he would walk
the round acreage of paradise.

3.

I've seen the diagrams
of loss on my grandfather's face,
and have stood with him
as he strained to see
the comet's dim smudge
for a second time.
I've thought of its ice
wrapped in fire
circling the century,
and its fine dust falling
beneath the ground glass
where all magic
yields up its molecules.

My grandparents have lapsed
into the scent of figs
and palm ash, the sound
of a screen door
slammed by wind, have lapsed
into the storied cornfields
of paradise, where no one
could look into the face of God
and live.

Meditation in a Ruined Churchyard

Though I've knelt at burnished altars
as prayer climbed the curling myrrh and candle smoke;
and though I've watched sunlight
blush and waver through stained glass,
believing the alchemy of wine and wafer;
though for years I contemplated the pulpit's Christ cast in
    plaster,
thorn, spear, and each nail driven through tendon,

these days my little remaining faith
is more likely to ripen among ruin—here, perhaps,
where fallen leaves heap themselves upon headstones,
where the chapel's been ransacked for brasswork and statues
and wind rattles a thicket's dominion beneath the trees.

It's necessary to praise this imperfection,
how the skilled hands of vandals
have left no window glass unshattered
and wasps build among broken tiles lining the rooftop.
What better reason to linger
where the long room's been emptied of its hymns
and water stains trace their blotched clouds across the ceiling?

This eloquent desolation needs no elegy.
So why lament the splintered pews piled beside the choir stall
or mourn the spent ribcage of rafters?
Let ivy's winding cloth
whelm the headless cherubs hunched along the brickwalk;
let gravestones fall to fireweed and thistle,
and let trumpet vine spiral and blossom
on the concrete bough where the lean God is nailed.